T0066274

THE ULTIMATE COLLECTION
WALTZES
AND OTHER SONGS IN 3/4 TIME
for the
UKULELE
89
FABULOUS FAVORITES

COMPILED & ARRANGED BY DICK SHERIDAN

To access audio visit:
www.halleonard.com/mylibrary

Enter Code
2206-8658-0260-8620

ISBN 978-1-57424-384-0
SAN 683-8022

Cover by James Creative Group

Copyright © 2019 CENTERSTREAM Publishing
P.O. Box 17878 - Anaheim Hills, CA 92817

www.centerstream-usa.com | centerstrm@aol.com | 714-779-9390

All rights for publication and distribution are reserved.
No part of this book may be reproduced in any form or by any Electronic or mechanical means including information storage and retrieval systems without permission in writing from the publisher, except by reviewers who may quote brief passages in review.

Circa 1916.

Table of Contents

WALTZES & SONGS

Alphabetical

AN INTRODUCTION
The Author Reflects

Perhaps you have to be of a certain age to remember those dance steps that were shown in magazines using diagrams of tiny shoes in black and white to indicate where to place the feet. One shoe represented the left foot, another the right foot. Then, in a prescribed pattern, those images would indicate where to place the feet for a particular dance. There was the Fox Trot, the Tango, the Lindy Hop. Certainly there was the Box Step alternating left and right feet to form an imaginary square.

Then there was the waltz. Ah, the waltz. One-Two-Three. One-Two-Three. Those foot prints gliding around to imagined Viennese music. Images that transcended numbered foot prints to become glittering ballrooms with sparkling crystal chandeliers, lovely ladies in flowing pastel gowns, fashionable men in elegant evening wear.

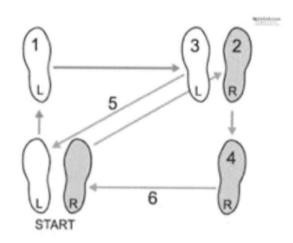

For most people it was the waltz that started their way to tripping the light fantastic. Many folks never got beyond the waltz. I can recall my father telling my mother, "Waltz faster, Bessie, it's a tango!" My sister learned to waltz by standing on our father's feet. For me it was the agony of choosing a partner in gym class, hopeful somebody who could teach me the basics.

I had a guitar teacher who also taught dancing. For me, a boy, he'd pull the studio blinds down so our lessons were not visible from the street and then run me through the basic steps dancing together. It was an awkward but innocent arrangement. When I got good enough he'd bring in his wife, and I knew that was a great relief for him as well as for me. As they say, that was back in the day. Women dancing with women was common and nobody thought a thing about it. But man to man was another matter. Times have changed. I was glad for the lessons which later held me in good stead with my high school girl friend. I was no Twinkle Toes, for sure, but I wasn't hesitant to put my best foot forward and head for the dance floor.

Scanning the trail of popular music for centuries, it seems fair to say that the waltz with its 3/4 time has contributed more than any other form of meter. From popular songs to classical instrumentals, the waltz has held sway and is the undisputed king.

No other form of music has proved more romantic than two hearts beating in three-quarter time. Ballads, operas, symphonies – all pay homage to the waltz, and it reigns supreme.

Where would the Irish be without their *"Casey would waltz with the strawberry blonde"* or the Germans and *Du, Du, Liegst Mir Im Herzen?* The "Merry Widow" opera would be flat and vacuous without its famous waltz of the same name. How deprived we'd be without Nelson Eddy and Jeanette McDonald singing *I'm Falling In Love With Someone* from Victor Herbert's 1935 operetta "Naughty Marietta" or even the *Anniversary Waltz* adapted by Al Jolson from the *Waves of the Danube* for his 1945 movie "The Jolson Story." Way "down under" in Australia, Banjo Patterson's *Waltzing Matilda* is nothing short of a national anthem,

For fans of PBS-TV there was the Masterpiece Theater theme *Rondeau* by French Baroque composer Jean-Joseph Mouret. Not to be outdone, Frederic Chopin added some of the most memorable piano waltzes ever written.

On the humorous side we find more waltzes. Allan Sherman came forth in 1963 with his Camp Granada song *Hello, Mudduh, Hello, Fadduh* with music based on Ponchielli's *Dance of the Hours*. And certainly not to be forgotten is Kermit The Frog playing a left-handed banjo and singing *The Rainbow Connection* from the "Muppet Movie" which was nominated Best Song in 1979.

But not all music in three-quarter time is a waltz. Take, for example, *The Star-Spangled Banner* or spirituals like *Amazing Grace* and *Rock of Ages*. I think you'd agree that few people would be inclined to waltz to *Happy Birthday* or *My Country 'Tis of Thee*.

The list of waltzes seems endless, and fortunately so. If all the waltzes ever written were combined into a single collection the size would be astronomical. So for us, the task of picking and choosing was equally daunting, but a fair and fun representation has emerged.

If any of your favorites has been omitted, we apologize. But there are many delightful substitutes to fill the gap. Among them are some of my personal choices: *Invitation to the Dance* by Carl Maria von Weber, first heard in a movie "The River" about a British family living in India shown during my college freshman orientation week. High on the list is Maurice Jarre's *Lara's Theme* from the movie "Doctor Zhivago" that remains an all-time favorite. No list would be complete without a hot dog, a beer in a paper cup, and *Take Me Out to the Ball Game*.

And there's the limericks parody of the Mexican folk songs *Cielto Lindo*, "Here comes the next verse that's worse than the other verse, so waltz me around again, Willie."

My Dixieland jazz band includes a number of waltzes in its repertoire. Irving Berlin's *Always* is a regular for dancing while *Together* -- recorded by all the greats from Louis Armstrong to Count Basie and Cliff "Ukulele Ike" Edwards -- makes for a fun song when we start it as a waltz and then swing into an upbeat 4/4.

Incidentally, all of these songs arranged for ukes tuned gCEA can also be played on the baritone uke. Just play the chord diagram and tablature; ignore the chord symbol (chord name) and the standard notation.

Whether you've got dancing shoes like Fred Astaire and Ginger Rogers from those memorable dance scenes in the 1940's movies, or even if you have two left feet like me and *Sweet Georgia Brown*, with the following ukulele waltzes you can waltz away to your heart's content and never have your feet touch the floor. And away we go, 1-2-3, 1-2-3!

"Two hearts beating in 3/4 time"

BLOW THE MAN DOWN

Ukulele tuning: gCEA

TRADITIONAL

2. As I was walking down Paradise Street,
'Way! Hey! Blow the man down!
A frolicsome damsel I chanced for to meet,
Give me some time to blow the man down.

3. She was round in the corner and bluff in the bow,
So I took in all sail and cried, "Way enough now!"

4. She says then to me, "Will you stand me a treat?"
"Delighted," says I, "for a charmer so sweet."

5. So I tailed her my flipper and took her in tow,
And yardarm to yardarm, away we did go.

6. I bought her a dinner, two shillings in town,
And trinkets and laces and bonnet and gown.

7. But I give you fair warning before we belay,
Don't ever take heed of what pretty girls say.

IN THE PINES

Ukulele tuning: gCEA

TRADITIONAL

CLEMENTINE

Ukulele tuning: gCEA

TRADITIONAL

♩ = 120

F

1. In a cav - ern, in a can - yon, ex - ca -

C7

vat - ing for a mine, lived a min - er, for - ty

F   **C7**   **F**

nin - er and his daught - er Clem - en - tine.

CHORUS: (Same melody as the verse)
Oh, my darling, oh, my darling,
Oh, my darling Clementine,
You are lost and gone forever,
Dreadful sorry, Clementine.

2. Light she was and like a fairy,
   And her shoes were number nine,
   Herring boxes without topses
   Sandals were for Clementine.
   CHORUS

3. Drove she ducklings to the water
   Ev'ry morning just at nine,
   Hit her foot against a splinter
   Fell into the foaming brine.
   CHORUS

4. Ruby lips above the water
   Blowing bubbles soft and fine,
   Alas for me I was no swimmer
   So I lost my Clementine.
   CHORUS

Note: "Forty Niner" is a nickname for a miner who took part in the gold rush of 1849. Gold was discovered that year at Sutter's Mill in Coloma, California, and the stampede of prospectors was on.

GOLD RUSH

DOWN IN THE VALLEY

Ukulele tuning: gCEA

TRADITIONAL

2. Roses love sunshine, violets love dew,
   Angels in heaven know I love you.
   Know I love you, love, know I love you,
   Angels in heaven know I love you.

3. If you don't love me, love whom you please,
   Throw your arms 'round me, give my heart ease.
   Etc.

4. Send me a letter, send it by mail,
   Send it in care of Birmingham jail.
   Etc.

5. Build me a castle forty feet high,
   So I can see you as you ride by.
   Etc.

When I lay down at night by a camp fire's light
And the work of the day is done
Then I wouldn't exchange my home on the range
For anything under the sun,
There's peace and rest out here in the west
Not found in your cities so grand
And when cowboys sing, the prairies ring
With music that I understand.

Carson J. Robison

HOUSE OF THE RISING SUN

Ukulele tuning: gCEA

TRADITIONAL

2. My mother was a tailor,
   She sewed my new blue jeans,
   My father was a gambling man
   Way down in New Orleans.

3. The only thing a gambler needs
   Is a suitcase and a trunk,
   The only time he's satisfied
   Is when he's on a drunk.

4. Oh, mother tell your children
   Don't do what I have done,
   Don't spend your life in misery
   In the House of the Rising Sun.

5. I've one foot on the platform,
   The other on the train,
   I'm going back to New Orleans
   To wear the ball and chain.

Circa 1922.

LITTLE MOHEE

Ukulele tuning: gCEA

TRADITIONAL

1. As I was a-walk - ing_____ up-on a fine day_____ I got aw-ful lone - some_____ as the day passed a - way._____ I sat down a-mus - ing_____ a - lone on the grass,_____ when who should sit by me,_____ but a sweet In - dian lass._____

2. She sat down beside me, took hold of my hand,
   Said, "You be a stranger and in a strange land."
   She asked me to marry and gave me her hand,
   Said, "My father's a chiefain all over this land."

3. " My father's a chieftain, and a ruler be he.
   I am his daughter and my name is Mohee."
   I answered and told her it never could be,
   I had my ain sweetheart in my ain country.

4. I had my ain sweetheart, and I knew she loved me.
   Her heart was as true as any Mohee.
   So I said, "I must leave you and goodbye, my dear.
   There's wind in my canvas and home I must steer."

5. At home with relations I tried for to see,
   But there wasn't another like my little Mohee.
   And the girl that I trusted proved untrue to me,
   So I sailed o'er the ocean to my little Mohee.

TAM PEARSE

Ukulele tuning: gCEA

TRADITIONAL

2. And when shall I see again my old grey mare,
   All along, down along, out along lea?
   By Friday noon or Saturday soon
   With Bill Brewer, Jan Stewer, etc.

3. Friday came and Saturday soon,
   All along, down along, out along lea,
   But Tam Pearse n'er did see his old grey mare come home
   With Bill Brewer, Jan Stewer, etc.

4. Tam he went to the top of the hill,
   All along, down along, out along lea,
   And he seed his old mare a-making her will
   With Bill Brewer, Jan Stewer, etc.

5. When the wind blows cold on the moor of a night,
   All along, down along, out along lea,
   Tam Pearse's grey mare appears ghastly white
   With Bill Brewer, Jan Stewer, etc.

WAYFARING STRANGER

Ukulele tuning: gCEA

TRADITIONAL

WAYFARING STRANGER

AWAY IN A MANGER

Ukulele tuning: gCEA

TRADITIONAL

THE CHERRY TREE CAROL

There are many variants to this old English carol, both in words and music. The origin of this version is uncertain, but the melody definitely has the feel of an American folk tune.

Ukulele tuning: gCEA

TRADITIONAL

2. As Joseph and Mary
   Walked through an orchard green,
   There were apples and cherries
   As thick as might be seen.

3. Then Mary spoke to Joseph,
   With words meek and mild,
   "Joseph, gather me some cherries,
   For I am with child," etc.

4. Then Jospeh flew in anger,
   In anger flew he,
   "Let the father of the baby
   Gather cherries for thee," etc.

5. O then besoke Jesus
   From the womb words spoke he,
   "Let my mother have some cherries,
   Bow down then, cherry tree," etc.

6. The cherry tree bow'd down then,
   Bow'd down to the ground,
   And Mary gathered cherries
   While Joseph stood around, etc.

7. As Joseph went a-walking,
   He heard angels sing,
   "This night there shall be born
   Our heavenly King," etc.

The Coventry Carol

Ukulele tuning: gCEA

TRADITIONAL

This hauntingly beautiful carol is often mistaken as a lullaby for the Infant Christ Child. In fact, it sadly laments the slaughter of the innocents as depicted in the second chapter of Matthew. Dating back to the 1500s, it was performed in Coventry, England, as part of the mystery play called the Pageant Of The Shearmen And Tailors. The final chord changes the prevailing minor sound to major in what is called a "Picardy third."

The Coventry Carol

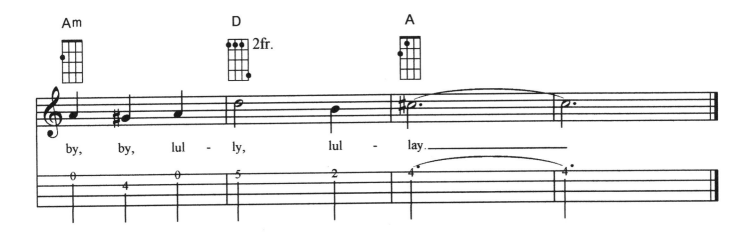

by, by, lul - ly, lul - lay.

2. O sisters too, how may we do,
   For to preserve this day,
   This poor youngling for whom we sing,
   By, by, lully, lullay?

3. Herod, the king, in his raging,
   Charg-ed he hath this day,
   His men of might, in his own sight,
   All children young to slay.

4. Then woe is me, poor child for thee!
   And ever mourn and say,
   For thy parting nor say nor sing
   By, by, lully lullay.

THE FIRST NOWELL

Ukulele tuning: gCEA

TRADITIONAL

THE FIRST NOWELL

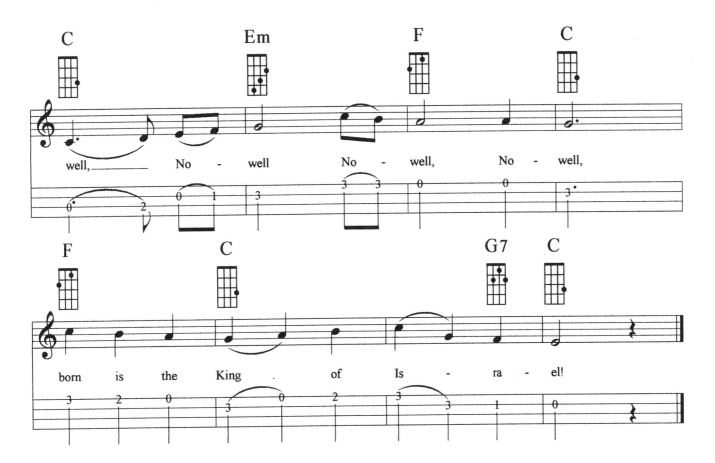

well,_____ No - well No - well, No - well,

born is the King of Is - ra - el!

Because the following three verses relate to the visit of the Magi, this carol is often associated with the Feast of the Epiphany, January 6. This is the "Twelfth Day of Christmas" and is sometimes referred to as Little Christmas. The date is observed by some religious traditions as Christmas Day itself.

2. They looked up and saw a star
Shining in the east beyond them far,
And to earth it gave great light,
And so it continued both day and night.
REFRAIN

3. This star drew nigh to the northwest,
O'er Bethlehem it took its rest,
And there it did both stop and stay
Right over the place where Jesus lay.
REFRAIN

4. Then entered in there Wise Men three,
Full rev'rently upon their knee,
And offer'd there in His presence
Their gold and myrrh and frankincense.
REFRAIN

GLOUCESTERSHIRE WASSAIL

Ukulele tuning: gCEA

TRADITIONAL

GLOUCESTERSHIRE WASSAIL

Wassail (Wes hal): Old English for "Be thou hale"

2. So here's to Cherry and to his right cheek,
   Pray God send our master a good piece of beef,
   And a good piece of beef that may we all see,
   With the wassailing bowl we'll drink to thee.

3. And here is to Dobbin and to his right eye,
   Pray god send our master a good Christmas pie,
   A good Christmas pie that may we all see,
   With our wassailing bowl we'll drink to thee.

4. So here is to Broad May and to her broad horn,
   May God send our master a good crop of corn,
   A good crop of corn that may we all see,
   With our wassailing bowl we'll drink to thee.

5. And here is to Filpail and to her left ear,
   God send our master a happy New Year,
   A happy New Year as e'er he did see,
   With our wassailing bowl we'll drink to thee.

6. Then here's to the maid in the lily white smock,
   Who trips to the door and slips back the lock,
   Who trips to the door and pulls back the pin,
   For to let us jolly wassailers in.

7. And here's to Colly and to her long tail,
   God send our master he never may fail,
   A bowl of strong beer, I pray you draw near,
   And our jolly wassail, it's then you shall hear.

Cherry and Dobbin are the names of horses.
Broad May, Filpail, and Colly are cows.

THE HOLLY AND THE IVY

Ukulele tuning: gCEA

TRADITIONAL

2. The holly bears a prickle,
   As sharp as any thorn,
   And Mary bore sweet Jesus Christ
   On Christmas day in the morn.

3. The holly bears a blossom,
   As sweet as any flower,
   And Mary bore sweet Jesus Christ
   To be our sweet savior.

4. The holly bears a berry,
   As red as any blood,
   And Mary bore sweet Jesus Christ
   To do poor sinners good.

WE WISH YOU A MERRY CHRISTMAS

Ukulele tuning: gCEA

TRADITIONAL

2. We all want some figgy pudding,
   We all want some figgy pudding,
   We all want some figgy pudding,
   And a cup of good cheer.

3. We won't go until we get some,
   We won't go until we get some,
   We won't go until we get some,
   So bring us some here.

CRADLE SONG

Ukulele tning: gCEA

JOHANNES BRAHMS
(1813 - 1888)

EMPEROR WALTZ

Ukulele tuning: gCEA

JOHANN STRAUSS

CLASSICAL

WALTZ
(Theme from the Opera "Faust")

Ukulele tuning: gCEA

CHARLES GOUNOD
(1818 - 1893)

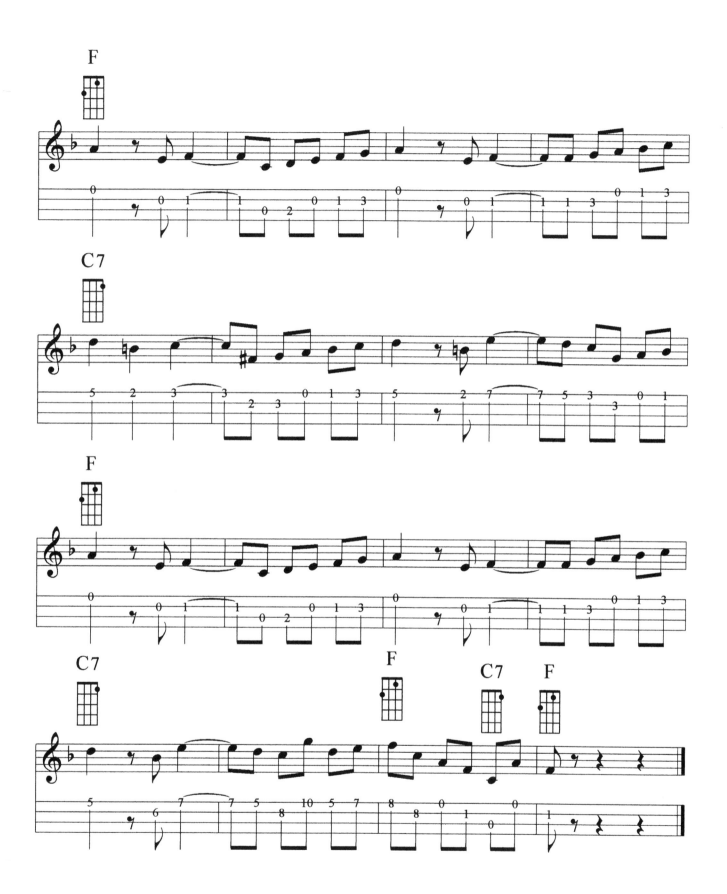

INVITATION TO THE DANCE

Ukulele tuning: gCEA

CARL MARIA von WEBER
(1786 - 1826)

MERRY WIDOW WALTZ

Ukulele tuning: gCEA

FRANZ LEHÁR
(1870-1948)

PRELUDE IN A
Op. 28, No. 7
(Transposed to F)

Ukulele tuning: gCEA

FRÉDÉRIC CHOPIN
(1810 - 1849)

MINUET
(From Anna Magdalena Notebook)

Ukulele tuning: gCEA

JOHANN SEBASTIAN BACH

(1685 - 1750)

MINUET IN G

Ukulele tuning: gCEA

LUDWIG van BEETHOVEN
(1770 - 1827)

SERENADE

Ukulele tuning: gCEA

FRANZ SCHUBERT
(1797 - 1828)

44

WALTZ IN A-FLAT
(Transposed to D)

Ukulele tuning: gCEA

JOHANNES BRAHMS
(1833 - 1897)

SKATERS' WALTZ

(Les Patineurs)

Ukulele tuning: gCEA

ÉMIL WALDTEUFEL
(1837 - 1915)

HOME ON THE RANGE

BREWSTER M. HIGLEY Ukulele tuning: gCEA DANIEL E. KELLEY

I RIDE AN OLD PAINT

Ukulele tuning: gCEA

TRADITIONAL

1.I ride an old Paint, I lead an old Dan, I'm

goin' to Mon - tan' for to throw the hoo - li - han. They

feed in the cool - ies, they wa - ter in the draw, their

tails are all mat - ted, their backs are all raw. Ride a -

CHORUS

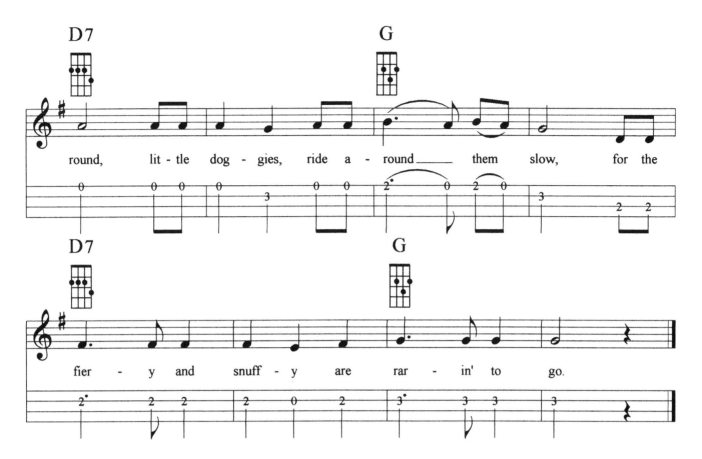

round, lit - tle dog - gies, ride a - round_____ them slow, for the

fier - y and snuff - y are rar - in' to go.

2. Old Bill Jones had two daughters and a song,
One went to Denver the other went wrong.
His wife she died in a poolroom fight,
And now he keeps singing from morning to night.
CHORUS

3. Oh, when I die, take my saddle from the wall,
Put it on my pony, lead him out of his stall,
Tie my bones to his back, turn our faces to the west,
And we'll ride the prairies that we love the best.
CHORUS

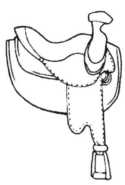

ON TOP OF OLD SMOKY

Ukulele tuning: gCEA

TRADITIONAL

2. For courting's a pleasure and parting's a grief,
   A false-hearted lover is worse than a thief.

3. A thief will just rob you and take what you have,
   A false-hearted lover will send you to your grave.

4. The grave will decay you and turn you to dust;
   Where is a young man a poor girl can trust?

5. They'll hug you and kiss you and tell you more lies
   Than the cross-ties on the railroad and the stars in the skies.

6. Come all you young maidens and listen to me,
   Never place your affections on a green willow tree.

7. The leaves they will wither and the roots they will die,
   You'll all be forsaken and never know why.

STREETS OF LAREDO

Ukulele tuning: gCEA

TRADITIONAL

2. "I see by your outfit that you are a cowboy,"
These words I did say as I boldly stepped by.
"Come sit down beside me and hear my sad story,
I'm shot in the breast and I know I must die.

3. "It was once in the saddle I used to go dashing,
Once in the saddle I used to go gay,
First to the card house and then down to Rosie's,
I'm shot in the breast and I'm dying today.

4. "Get six jolly cowboys to carry my coffin,
Get six pretty maidens to carry my pall,
Put bunches of roses all over my coffin,
Roses to deaden the clods as they fall.

5. "Oh, beat the drum slowly and play the fife lowly,
Play the dead march as you carry me along.
Take me to the green valley and lay the sod o'er me,
For I'm a young cowboy and I know I've done wrong."

SWEET BETSY FROM PIKE

Ukulele tuning: gCEA

TRADITIONAL

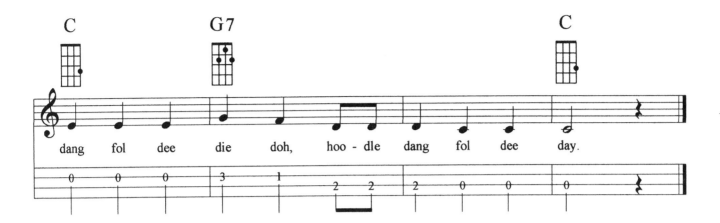

dang   fol   dee   die   doh,   hoo - dle   dang   fol   dee   day.

2. One evening quite early they camped on the Platte,
   Down by the road on a green shady flat,
   Where Betsy, sore-fotted, lay down with repose,
   With wonder Ike gazed on his Pike County rose.

3. They soon reached the desert where Betsy gave out,
   Down in the sand she lay rolling about,
   While Ike half distracted looked on with surprise
   Saying "Do get up, Betsy, you'll get sand in your eyes."

4. Long Ike and sweet Betsy attended a dance,
   Ike wore a pair of his Pike County pants,
   Betsy was dressed up in ribbons and wings,
   Ike said, "You're an angel but where are your wings?"

5. A miner comes up, says "Will you dance with me?"
   "I will, you old hoss, if you don't make too free.
   Don't dance me too hard, do you want to know why,
   Gosh darn ye I'm chucked up with strong alkali."

6. The Shanghai ran off and the cattle all died,
   That morning the last piece of bacon was fried,
   Poor Ike was discouraged and Betsy got mad,
   The dog drooped his tail and looked wondrously sad.

WHOOPEE TI YI YO
GET ALONG, LITTLE DOGGIES

Ukulele tuning: gCEA

TRADITIONAL

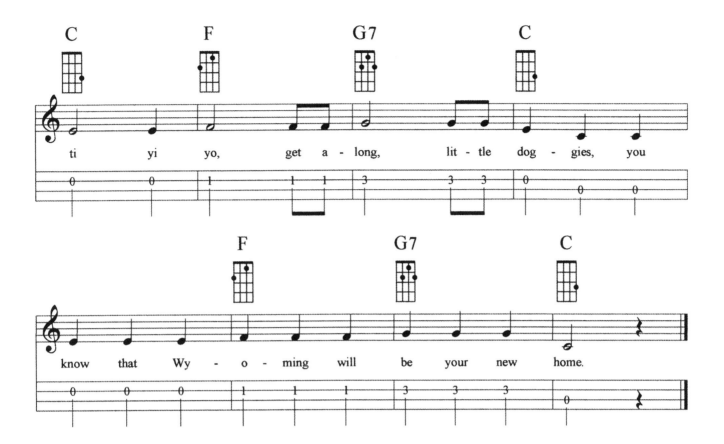

ti yi yo, get a - long, lit - tle dog - gies, you know that Wy - o - ming will be your new home.

2. It's early in spring that we round up the doggies,
   And mark 'em and brand 'em and lop off their tails.
   We round up our horses and load the chuck wagon,
   And then throw the doggies out on the trail.
   CHORUS

3. It's whoopin' and yellin' and a-drivin' them doggies,
   Oh, how I wish that you would go on.
   It's a-whoopin' and punchin' and go on-a, little doggies,
   For you know that Wyoming will be your new home.
   CHORUS

4. Some cowboys go up on the trail just for pleasure,
   But that's where they get it most terribly wrong,
   For nobody knows what trouble they give us,
   As we go driving them doggies along.
   CHORUS

A BIRD IN A GILDED CAGE

ARTHUR J. LAMB

Ukulele tuning: gCEA

HARRY VON TILZER

A BIRD IN A GUILDED CAGE

63

AFTER THE BALL

Ukulele tuning: gCEA

CHARLES K. HARRIS

ALICE BLUE GOWN

JOSEPH McCARTHY   HARRY TIERNEY

Ukulele tuning: gCEA

ALICE BLUE GOWN

The color Alice Blue -- an icy shade of pale blue - is said to have been so named because of the gowns of that color favored by Alice Roosevelt Longworth, daughter of President Theodore Roosevelt.

man - ner of fash - ion I'd frown,_____ and the

world seem'd to smile all a - round._____ Till it

wilt - ed I wore it, I'll al - ways a - dore it, my

sweet lit - tle Al - ice blue gown._____

THE BOWERY

CHARLES H. HOYT

Ukulele tuning: gCEA

PERCY GAUNT

DAISY BELL
(A Bicycle Built For Two)

Ukulele tuning: gCEA

HARRY DACRE

I'M FOREVER BLOWING BUBBLES

Ukulele tuning: gCEA

JAAN KENBROVIN
JOHN WILLIAM KELLETTE

IN THE GOOD OLD SUMMERTIME

Ukulele tuning: gCEA

REN SHIELDS

GEORGE EVANS

IN THE GOOD OLD SUMMERTIME

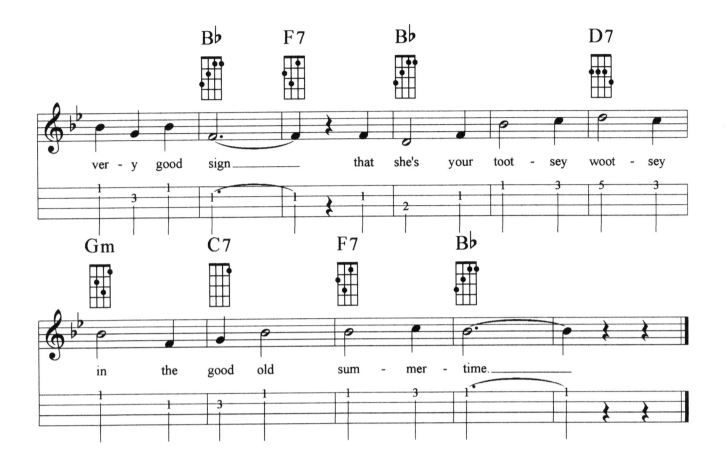

ver - y good sign_____ that she's your toot - sey woot - sey

in the good old sum - mer - time._____

IN THE SHADE OF THE OLD APPLE TREE

HARRY WILLIAMS

Ukulele tuning: gCEA

EGBERT VAN ALSTYNE

MY BUDDY

Ukulele tuning: gCEA

WALTER DONALDSON &GUS KAHN

SCHOOL DAYS

Ukulele tuning: gCEA

WILL D. COBB

GUS EDWARDS

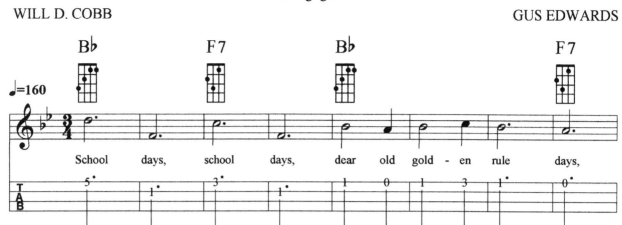

School days, school days, dear old gold - en rule days,

read - in' and 'rit - in' and 'rith - me - tic,

taught to the tune of a hic 'ry stick.

You were my queen in cal - i - co,

ASH GROVE

Ukulele tuning: gCEA

TRADITIONAL WELSH

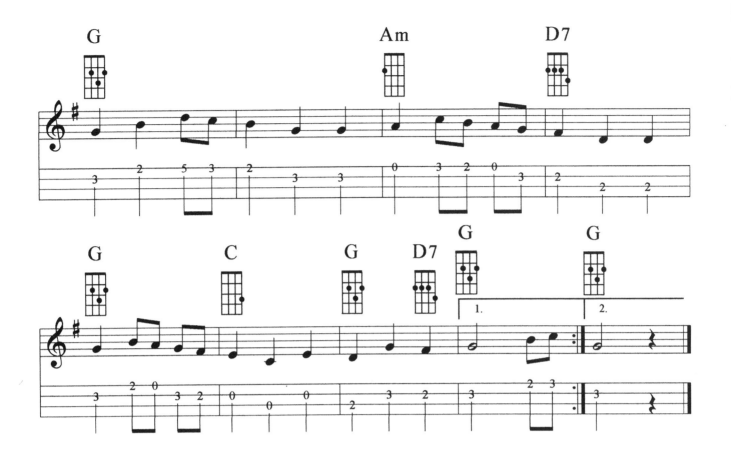

*This traditional waltz from Wales can be found with other beautiful tunes
in Centerstream's publication "Celtic Songs for the Tenor Banjo."*

CIELITO LINDO

Ukulele tuning: gCEA

TRADITIONAL MEXICAN

FLOW GENTLY, SWEET AFTON

ROBERT BURNS Ukulele tuning: gCEA TRADITIONAL

FLOW GENTLY, SWEET AFTON

DU, DU LIEGST MIR IM HERZEN

Ukulele tuning: gCEA

TRADITIONAL GERMAN

Du, du liegst mir im Her - zen,

di, du liegst mir im Sinn;

du, du liegst mir im Her - zen

weisst nichct wie gut ich dir bin.

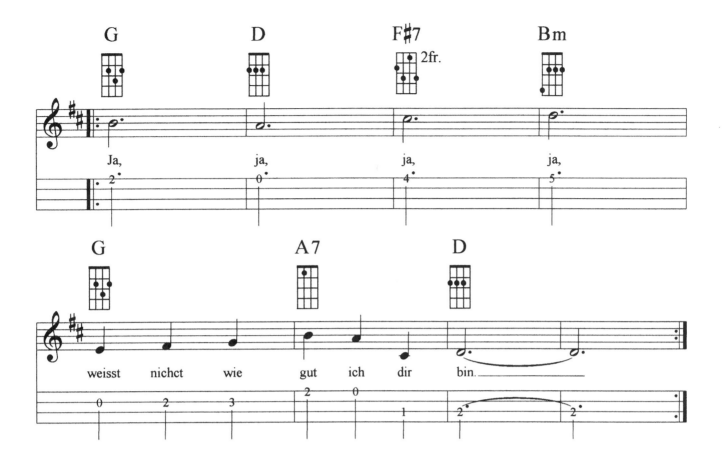

Ja, ja, ja, ja,

weisst nichct wie gut ich dir bin.

HINE MA TOV

Ukulele tuning: gCEA

TRADITIONAL JEWISH

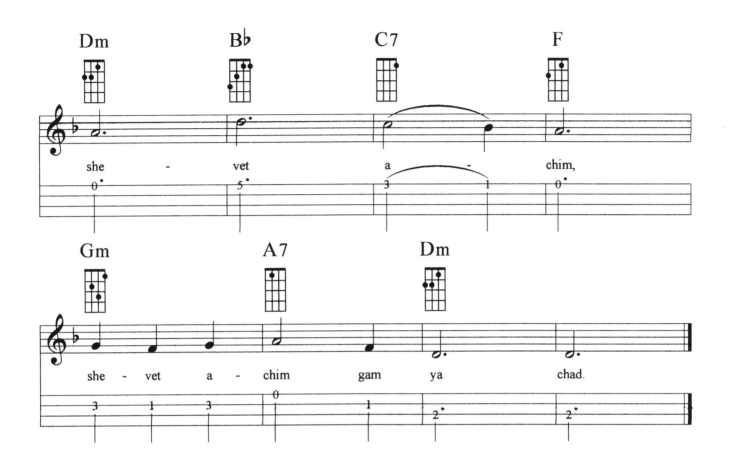

she - vet a - chim,

she - vet a - chim gam ya chad.

JUANITA

Ukulele tuning: gCEA

TRADITIONAL SPANISH

CHO: Ni - ta! Jua___ ni - ta! Ask thy soul if we should part!

Ni - ta! Jua - ni - ta! Lean thou on my heart.

2. When in thy dreaming, moons like these shall shine again,
And daylight beaming, prove thy dreams are vain.
Wilt thou not, relenting, for thy absent lover sigh,
In thy heart consenting to a prayer gone by.
CHORUS

O DU LIEBER, AUGUSTIN

Ukulele tuning:gCEA

TRADITIONAL AUSTRIAN

♩=130

O   du lieb - er Au - gus - tin,   Au - gus - tun,   Au - gus - tin.

O   du lieb - er Au - gus - tin, al - les ist hin.

Geld   ist weg, Mäd'l ist weg, al - les hin, Au - gus - tin,

O   du lieb - er Au - gus - tin, al - les - ist hin.

OVER THE WAVES
(Sobre Las Olas)

Ukulele tuning: gCEA

JUVENTINO ROSAS

No circus would be complete without trapeze acrobats sailing through the air to the accompaniment of this tune.

DARK EYES

Ukulele tuning: gCEA

TRADITIONAL RUSSIAN

Circa 1916.

AN IRISH LULLABY

Ukulele tuning: gCEA

JAMES ROYCE SHANNON

AN IRISH LULLABY

Chorus: Too ra loo ra loo ral,_____ too ra loo ra li,

too ra loo ra loo ral,_____ hush, now don't you cry. Oh,

Too ra loo ra loo ral,_____ too ra loo ra li,

too ra loo ra loo ral, that's an I - rish lul - la - by.

Verse 2.
Oft in dreams I wander to that little cot again.
I feel her arms a-hugging me as when she held me then.
And I hear her voice a-humming to me as in days of yore,
When she used to rock me fast asleep outside the cabin door.
CHORUS

LITTLE ANNIE ROONEY

Ukulele tuning: gCEA

MICHAEL NOLAN

She's my sweet - heart, I'm her beau,_____ she's my An - nie,_____ I'm her Joe._____ Soon we'll mar - ry,_____ nev - er_____ to part,_____ Lit - tle An - nie Roon - ey_____ is my sweet - heart._____

SWEET ROSIE O'GRADY

Ukulele tuning: gCEA

Words and music by
MAUD NUGENT

THE BAND PLAYED ON

Ukulele tuning: gCEA

JOHN F. PALMER

CHARLES B. WARD

THE BAND PLAYED ON

MOLLY MALONE

Ukulele tuning: gCEA

TRADITIONAL

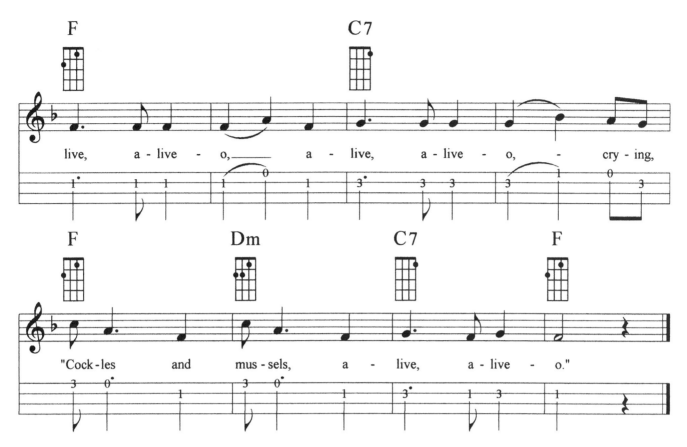

live, a - live - o,_____ a - live, a - live - o, - cry - ing,

"Cock - les and mus - sels, a - live, a - live - o."

2. She was a fishmonger, and sure 'tis no wonder,
   For so were her mother and father before.
   They wheeled their wheelbarrows
   Through streets broad and narrow, crying
   "Cockles and mussels, alive, alive-o."
         Alive, alive-o, alive, a-live-o, crying
         "Cockles and mussels, alive, alive-o."

3. She died of a fever, and no one could save her,
   And that was the end of sweet Molly Malone.
   Now her ghost wheels her barrow
   Through streets broad and narrow, crying
   "Cockles and mussels, alive, alive-o."
         Alive, alive-o, alive, alive-o, crying
         "Cockles and mussels, alive, alive-o."

NELLIE KELLY, I LOVE YOU

Ukulele tuning: gCEA

GEORGE M. COHAN

PEGGY O'NEIL

Ukulele tuning: gCEA

Words and Music by
HARRY PEASE, ED. G. NELSON, and GILBERT DODGE

WHEN IRISH EYES ARE SMILING

Ukulele tuning: gCEA

CHAUNCEY OLCOTT
and GEORGE GRAFF, JR.

ERNEST R. BALL

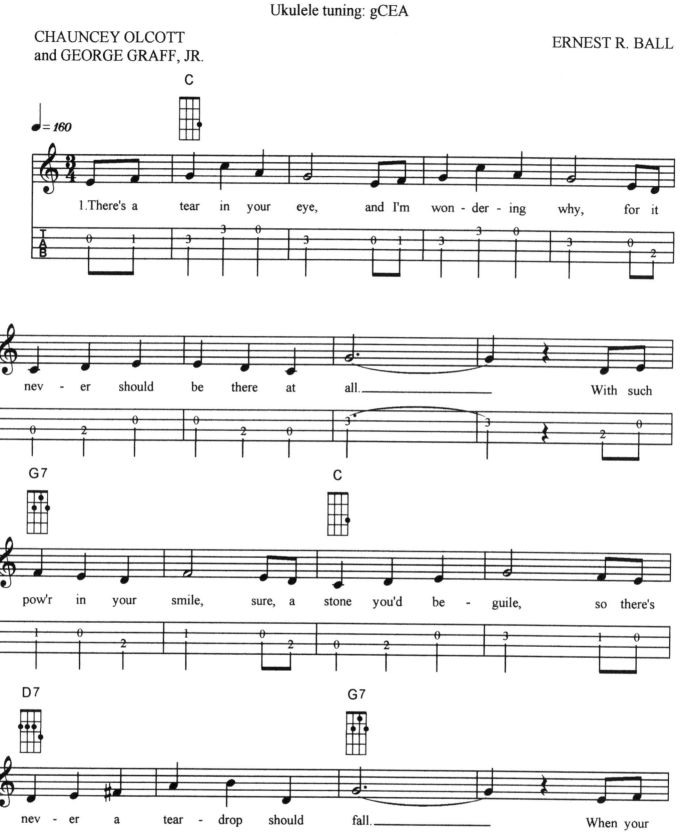

1.There's a tear in your eye, and I'm won - der - ing why, for it

nev - er should be there at all._____ With such

pow'r in your smile, sure, a stone you'd be - guile, so there's

nev - er a tear - drop should fall._____ When your

WHEN IRISH EYES ARE SMILING

109

WHEN IRISH EYES ARE SMILING

WHEN IRISH EYES ARE SMILING

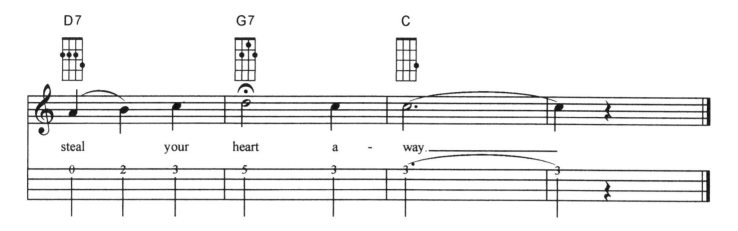

steal   your   heart   a -   way.

2. For your smile is a part of the love in your heart,
And it makes even sunshine more bright;
Like the linnet's sweet song, crooning all the day long,
Comes your laughter so tender and light.
For the springtime of life is the sweetest of all,
There is ne'er a real care or regret;
And while springtime is ours,
Throughout all of youth's hours,
Let us smile each chance that we get.
CHORUS

Surely it is not an exaggeration to say that "When Irish Eyes Are Smiling" is probably the most popular of all Irish-American songs. Its co-lyricist, Chancellor "Chauncey" Olcott, was the personification of the consummate Irishman despite having been born in Buffalo, New York. But Olcott's ancestry was Irish and he paid tribute to it with stage performances, Broadway musicals he produced, and songs and lyrics he wrote -- all with an Irish theme. His singular efforts and collaborations can be found not only in "When Irish Eyes Are Smiling, but also in "My Wild Irish Rose," and "Mother Machree," to name just a few. Ernest Ball, although not Irish himself, wrote the music to many of these songs and the scores of Olcott's shows, as well as "A Little Bit Of Heaven" and the memorable "Let The Rest Of The World Go By."

Flamboyant State Senator James Walker, known as Dapper Jimmy Walker, asked Ball to write music for some lyrics he had penned. The result was "Will You Love Me In December As You Do In May" which became a hit song and a campaign vehicle for Walker's successful run for Mayor of New York City. He was elected in 1926 and held office until 1932.

Ball's grandson Ernie Ball is well known for his popular line of guitar and bass strings.

MY WILD IRISH ROSE

Ukulele tuning: gCEA

CHAUNCEY OLCOTT

THE SATURDAY EVENING POST

June 14, 1930

10c. in Canada

5cts.

Julian Street—Isaac F. Marcosson—David Lawrence—Everett Rhodes Castle
Marjory S. Douglas—Ben Ames Williams—Anne Cameron—Julius H. Barnes

I'M FALLING IN LOVE WITH SOMEONE

Ukulele tuning: gCEA

RIDA JOHNSON YOUNG

VICTOR HERBERT

I'M FALLING IN LOVE WITH SOMEONE

HOW GREAT IS THE PLEASURE

Ukulele tuning: gCEA

HENRY HARRNGTON (1727-1816)

Sweet, sweet, how sweet the ___ de - light, ___ when

har - mo - ny, sweet har - mo - ny and love ___ do u - nite!

Childhood film star Shirly Temple.

IF I HAD MY WAY

LOU KLEIN

Ukulele tuning: gCEA

JAMES KENDIS

IF YOU WERE THE ONLY GIRL IN THE WORLD

Ukulele tuning: gCEA

CLIFFORD GREY

NAT D. AYER

LET THE REST OF THE WORLD GO BY

KEIRN BRENNAN

Ukulele tuning: gCEA

ERNEST R. BALL

LET ME CALL YOU SWEETHEART

Ukulele tuning: gCEA

BETH SLATER WHITSON

LEO FRIEDMAN

LOVE'S OLD SWEET SONG

Ukulele tuning: gCEA

G. CLIFTON BINGHAM

JAMES LYNAM MOLLOY

MY BONNIE LIES OVER THE OCEAN

Ukulele tuning: gCEA

TRADITIONAL

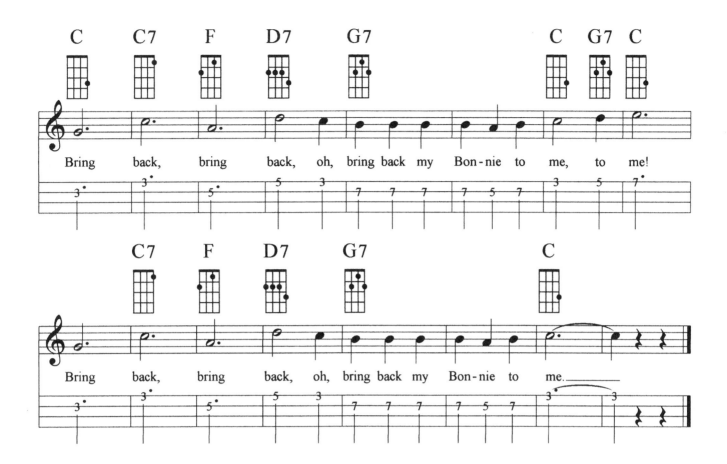

Bring back, bring back, oh, bring back my Bon-nie to me, to me!

Bring back, bring back, oh, bring back my Bon-nie to me._____

Verse 2. Oh, blow the winds over the ocean,
Oh, blow the winds over the sea,
Oh, blow the winds over the ocean,
And bring back my Bonnie to me.

MY GAL SAL

Ukulele tuning: gCEA

PAUL DRESSER

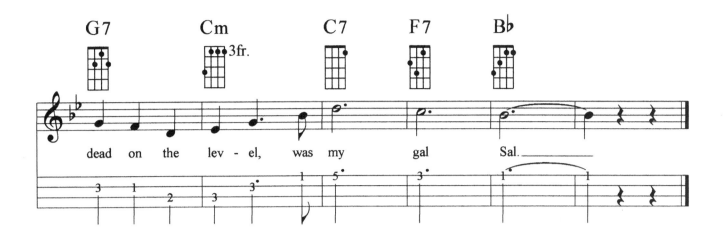

dead   on   the   lev - el,   was   my   gal   Sal._____

Circa 1960.

TILL WE MEET AGAIN

Ukulele tuning: gCEA

RAYMOND B. EAGAN

RICHARD A. WHITING

130

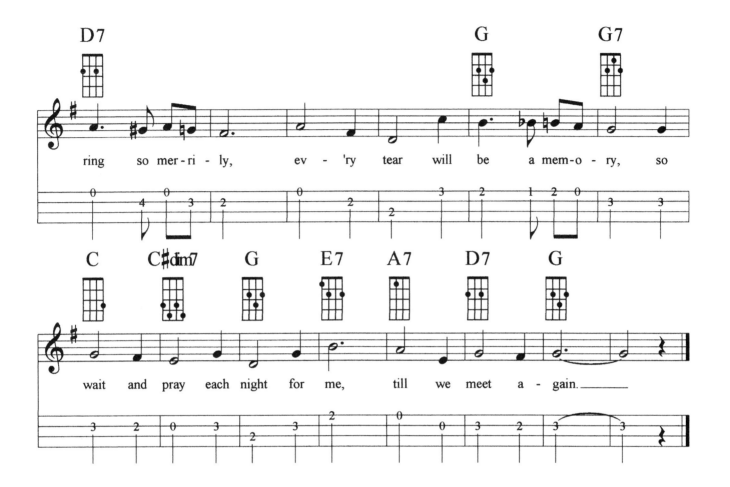

I WONDER WHO'S KISSING HER NOW

WILL M. HOUGH
& FRANK R. ADAMS

Ukulele tuning: gCEA

JOSEPH E. HOWARD
& HAROLD ORLOB

I won-der who's kiss-ing her now,___

won-der who's teach-ing her how,___

won-der who's look-ing in-to her eyes,

breath - ing sighs, tell - ing lies. I

SWEET GENEVIEVE

Ukulele tuning: gCEA

HENRY TUCKER

YOU TELL ME YOUR DREAM,
I'LL TELL YOU MINE

SEYMOUR RICE and
ALBERT H. BROWN

Ukulele tuning: gCEA

CHARLES N. DANIELS

ABDULLAH BULBUL AMIR

Ukulele tuning: gCEA

Traditional

ABDULLAH BULBUL AMIR

These lyrics are an extraction from much longer ones that can be found on the Internet.

This son of the desert in battle aroused,
Could split twenty men on his spear.
A terrible creature when sober or soused
Was Abdullah Bulbul Amir.

Now the heroes were plenty and well known to fame
Who fought in the ranks of the Czar,
But the bravest of these was a man by the name
Of Ivan Skavinsky Skivar.

He could dance the fandango, play poker or pool,
And strum on the Spanish guitar;
In fact, quite the cream of the Muscovite team
Was Ivan Skavinsky Skivar.

One day this bold Russian had shouldered his gun,
And donned his most truculent sneer,
Downtown he did go where he trod on the toe
Of Abdullah Bulbul Amir.

"Young man," quoth Abdullah, "has life grown so dull
That you're anxious to end your career?
Do you not know you have trod on the toe
Of Abullah Bulbul Amir?"

"So take your last look at the sunshine and brook,
And send your regrets to the Czar,
For by this I imply, you are going to die,
Mr. Ivan Skavinsky Skivar."

Said Ivan, "My friend, your remarks in the end
Will avail you but little, I fear;
For you ne'er will survive to repeat them alive,
Mr. Abdullah Bulbul Amir."

They parried and thrust, they sidestepped and cussed,
Of blood they spilled a great part;
The philologist blokes, who seldom crack jokes,
Said that hash was first made on that spot.

There's a tomb rises up where the Blue Danube rolls,
And graved there in characters clear
Are "Strangers, when passing, oh pray for the soul
Of Abdullah Bulbul Amir."

THE FLYING TRAPEZE

(The Man on the Flying Trapeze)

GEORGE LEYBOURNE

Ukulele tuning: gCEA

ALFRED LEE

Once I was hap-py but now I'm for-lorn, like an old coat that is tat-tered and torn, left on this wide world to fret and to mourn, be-trayed bu a maid in her teens. He'd

IN MY MERRY OLDSMOBILE

VINCENT BRYAN   Ukulele tuning: gCEA   GUS EDWARDS

IN MY MERRY OLDSMOBILE

How many great cars have hit the road then bit the dust! Like the Oldsmobile, gone is Plymouth, Pontiac, Studebaker and Mercury. Gone too but well forgotten is the Edsel, Henry J, and Kaiser-Frazer. Oldsmobile flourished from the early 1900s until its demise in 2004.

church we'll swift - ly steal._____ then our

wed - ding bells will peal,_____ you can

go as far as you like with

me in my mer - ry Olds - mo - bile._____

TAKE ME OUT TO THE BALL GAME

Ukulele tuning: gCEA

JACK NORWORTH   ALBERT VON TILZER

TAKE ME OUT TO THE BALL GAME

It's ironic that neither Jack Norworth or Albert Von Tilzer had ever seen a ball game when they wrote this song in 1908. It is credited as one of the 365 top songs of the 20th Century.

THE WHIFFENPOOF SONG

MEADE MINNIGERODE
GEORGE S. POMEROY

Ukulele tuning: gCEA

ANONYMOUS

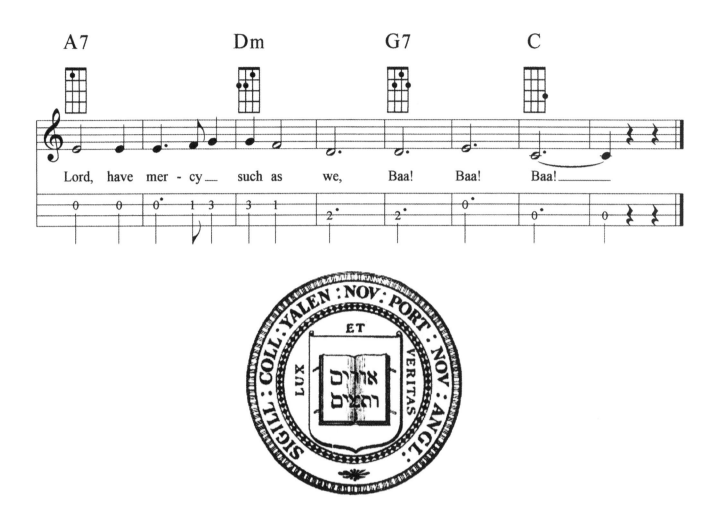

The Whiffenpoofs is a collegiate male singing group established in 1909 at Yale University.

HAPPY BIRTHDAY

Ukulele tuning: gCEA

TRADITIONAL

Circa 1910.

AMERICA
(My Country 'Tis of Thee)

SAMUEL F. SMITH   Ukulele tuning: gCEA   TRADITIONAL

This melody is the same as "God Save the Queen" the national anthem of the United Kingdom.

2. My native country, thee,
   Land of the noble free,
   Thy name I love;
   I love thy rocks and rills,
   Thy woods and templed hills,
   My heart with rapture thrills
   Like that above.

3. Let music swell the breeze,
   And ring from all the trees
   Sweet freedom's song;
   Let mortal tongues awake,
   Let all that breathe partake;
   Let rocks their silence break,
   The sound prolong.

4. Our fathers' God, to thee,
   Author of liberty,
   To thee we sing:
   Long may our land be bright
   With freedom's holy light;
   Protect us by thy might,
   Great God, our king.

THE STAR-SPANGLED BANNER
The National Anthem of the United States of America

FRANCIS SCOTT KEY   Ukulele tuning: gCEA   JOHN STAFFORD SMITH

IN OLD NEW YORK

HENRY BLOSSOM   Ukulele tuning: gCEA   VICTOR HERBERT

MEET ME IN ST. LOUIS, LOUIS

ANDREW B. STERLING

KERRY MILLS

Ukulele tuning: gCEA

154

The acquition of the Louisiana Territory from France was celebrated 100 years later in 1904 by the
St. Louis World's Fair held in St. Louis, Missouri. Officially known as the Louisiana Purchase Expo-
sition, the Fair itself was remembered in the 1944 movie "Meet Me In St. Louis"starring Judy Garland.

THE MISSOURI WALTZ

J.R. SHANNON

FREDERIC KNIGHT LOGAN

Ukulele tuning: gCEA

ON MIAMI SHORE

WILLIAM LE BARON

VICTOR JACOBI

On the gold - en sands of old Mi - am - i shore there I al - ways find a girl whom I a - dore

How well I remember Arthur Godfrey -- relaxed, easygoing host of radio and TV shows -- singing this song while accompanying himself on a baritone ukulele. His radio show "Arthur Godfrey Time" ran from the 1940s to the 70s, a remarkable span of almost 30 years!

THE SIDEWALKS OF NEW YORK

Ukulele tuning: gCEA

JAMES W. BLAKE
CHARLES B. LAWLOR

AMAZING GRACE

Ukulele tuning: gCEA

TRADITIONAL

2. 'Twas grace that taught my heart to fear,
   And grace my fears relieved.
   How precious did that grace appear,
   The hour I first believed.

3. The Lord has promised good to me,
   His word my hope secures.
   He will my shield and portion be
   As long as life endures.

4. Through many dangers, toils, and snares,
   I have already come.
   'Tis grace has brought me safe thus far,
   And grace will lead me home.

5. When we've been there ten thousand years,
   Bright shining as the sun,
   We've no less days to sing God's praise,
   Than when we'd first begun.

DONA NOBIS PACEM

Ukulele tuning: gCEA

TRADITIONAL

Give us peace

The song, which is divided into three sections, is typically sung as a "round" by a trio of three voices. After all voices sing the entire song, Voice #1 sings the first section and moves to the second section. As Voice #1 is singing the second section Voice #2 simultaenously sings the first section. Voices #1 and #2 move to the next section and Voice #3 sings the first section. In a "follow the leader" sequence each voice advances to the next section, all singing together in overlapping harmony, around and around.

HOLY GOD, WE PRAISE THY NAME

Ukulele tuning: gCEA

TRADITIONAL

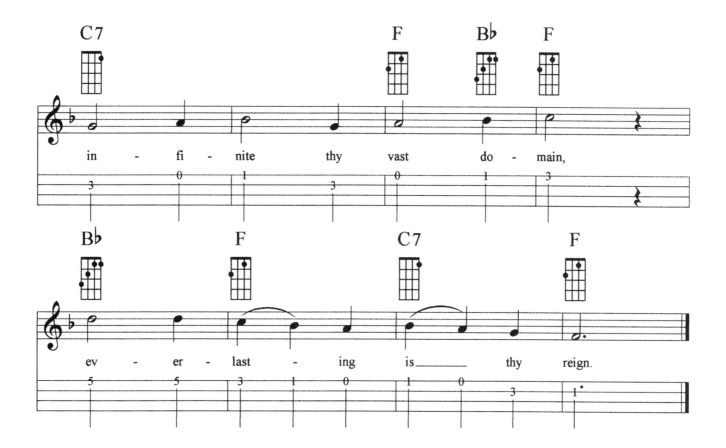

in - fi - nite thy vast do - main,

ev - er - last - ing is_____ thy reign.

2. Hark! the loud celestial hymn,
   Angels choirs above are raising!
   Cherubim and Seraphim
   In unceasing chorus praising;
   Fill the heav'ns with sweet accord:
   Holy, holy, holy Lord!

3. Holy Father, Holy Son,
   Holy Spirit, three we name thee,
   While in essence only one,
   Undivided God we claim thee:
   And adoring bend the knee,
   While we own the mystery.

PRAISE TO THE LORD

TRADITIONAL

Ukulele tuning: gCEA

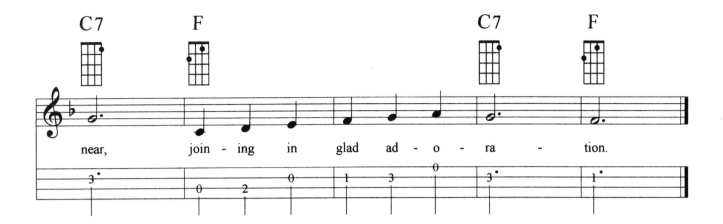

near,   join - ing   in   glad   ad - o - ra - tion.

2. Praise to the Lord,
   who doth prosper thy work and defend thee.
   Surely his goodness and mercy
   Shall daily attend thee.
   Ponder anew what the Almighty can do,
   Who with his love doth befriend thee.

3. Praise to the Lord,
   O let all that is in me adore him.
   All that has life and breath
   Come now in praises attend thee.
   Let the Amen sound from his people again,
   Now as we worship before him.

ROCK OF AGES

Ukulele tuning: gCEA

TRADITIONAL

2. While I draw this fleeting breath,
When mine eyes shall close in death,
When I rise to worlds unknown
And behold Thee on Thy throne,
Rock of ages, cleft for me,
Let me hide myself in Thee.

WE GATHER TOGETHER

Ukulele tuning: gCEA

TRADITIONAL

UKULELE BOOKS

**THE LOW G STRING
TUNING UKULELE**
by Ron Middlebrook
00001534.......................... $19.99

**63 COMICAL SONGS
FOR THE UKULELE**
Fun for all ages!
arr. Dick Sheridan
00279888.......................... $15.00

NEW

FINGERSTYLE UKULELE 2
by Kev Rones
00283176.......................... $17.99

GREAT UKULELE BOOKS FROM

ASAP UKULELE
*Learn How to Play
the Ukulele Way*
by Ron Middlebrook
00001359............................$14.99

**ASAP CHORD SOLOS FOR
THE BARITONE UKULELE**
by Dick Sheridan
00145630...........................$19.99

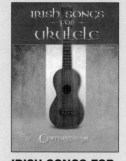

**IRISH SONGS FOR
UKULELE**
by Dick Sheridan
00103153 ....$15.99

**UKULELE BLUES - THE
UKULELE PLAYER'S GUIDE
TO THE BLUES**
by Kevin Rones
00141051 Book/CD $19.99

**FIDDLE TUNES FOR
BARITONE UKULELE**
by Dick Sheridan
00153260 Book/Audio $19.99

A

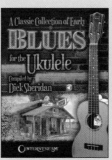

**CLASSIC COLLECTION OF
EARLY BLUES FOR THE
UKULELE**
compiled by Dick Sheridan
00216670 Book/Audio $15.99

**CLASSICAL MUSIC FOR
THE UKULELE**
arranged by Dick Sheridan
00138276 Book/CD $19.99

**KEV'S
QUICKSTART
FOR FINGERSTYLE
UKULELE**
by Kevin Rones
00001590 Book/CD Pack...$17.99

HALLELUJAH UKULELE
*19 of the Best and Most
Beloved Hymns & Spiritualsy*
by Dick Sheridan
00122113........................... $12.99

Order today! Call **1-714-779-9390** • **orders@centerstream-usa.com**

MORE UKULELE BOOKS

**THE AMAZING
INCREDIBLE SHRINKING
UKULELE**
*by Thornton Cline, Illustrations
by Susan Oliver*
00194560............................. $9.99

FUN SONGS FOR UKULELE
by Ron Middlebrook
00000407........................... $14.95

**KID'S UKE – UKULELE
ACTIVITY FUN BOOK**
Kev's Learn & Play Series
by Kevin Rones
00173015 (Ages 4-8) $11.99

UKULELE 101
*The Fun & Easy Ukulele
Method*
by Kevin Rones
00119896 Book/CD $17.99

**UKULELE
FOR COWBOYS**
by Ron Middlebrook
00000408 Ukulele $14.99

**UKULELE
SONGBOOK**
compiled by Ron Middlebrook
00000248.............................$9.99

**YULETIDE
FAVORITES FOR UKULELE**
*A Treasury of Christmas
Hymns, Carols & Songs*
by Dick Sheridan
00109749............................ $9.99

**CHRISTMAS
UKULELE,
HAWAIIAN STYLE**
00000472 Book/CD $19.99

**KEV'S QUICKSTART
UKULELE
CHRISTMAS SONGS**
arr. Kevin Rones
00110195 ....$9.99

Order today! Call **1-714-779-9390** • **orders@centerstream-usa.com**
Centerstream is distributed by Hal Leonard

CENTERSTREAM®   **1-714-779-9390**

UKULELE CHORDS
Plus Intros and Endings
by Ron Middlebrook
00000246............................$3.50

THE SONGS OF GILBERT & SULLIVAN FOR UKULELE
arr. Dick Sheridan
00156013........................... $19.99

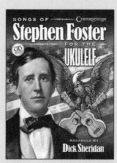

THE SONGS OF STEPHEN FOSTER FOR THE UKULELE
by Dick Sheridan
00145692 Book/CD $16.99

COLLEGE FIGHT SONGS & ALMA MATERS FOR UKULELE
by Dick Sheridan
00124458........................... $15.99

NAUTICAL SONGS FOR THE UKULELE
by Dick Sheridan
00129924........................... $15.99

THE SONGS OF TIN PAN ALLEY FOR UKULELE
arr. Dick Sheridan
00156812 Book/Audio....... $19.99

LOVE SONGS FOR UKULELE
by Dick Sheridan
00119342........................... $12.99

THE SONGS OF THE CIVIL WAR FOR UKULELE
by Dick Sheridan
00001588........................... $14.99

ULTIMATE LIT'L UKULELE CHORDS, PLUS
by Kahuna Uke
00001351 9 x 6...................$7.99

Go to **centerstream-usa.com** for complete descriptions of these titles.

More Great Books from Dick Sheridan...

CELTIC SONGS FOR THE TENOR BANJO
37 Traditional Songs and Instrumentals
by Dick Sheridan

Jigs & reels, hornpipes, airs, dances and more are showcased in this exciting 37 collection drawn from Ireland, Scotland, Wales, Cornwall, Brittany and the Isle of Man. Each traditional song – with its lilting melody and rich accompaniment harmony – has been carefully selected and presented for tenor banjo in both note form and tablature with chord symbols and diagrams. Lyrics and extra verses are included for many songs. Includes: All Through The Night, Blackbird Will You Go, The Campbells Are Coming, Garry Owen, Harvest Home, O'Gallaher's Frolics, Saddle The Pony, Swallow Tail Jig and many more.
00122477...$14.99

LOVE SONGS FOR UKULELE
37 Love Songs in All
by Dick Sheridan

Romance is in the air, and here to prove it are 37 of the best and most enduring love songs ever! Here are romantic treasures from the musical theater; whimsical novelty numbers; ballads of both true and false love; songs for sweethearts, lovers and hopefuls; sad songs of longing and heartbreak; and barbershop favorites. The creative ukulele arrangements in notes, tab & chords make each song rewarding and fun to play. Includes: Beautiful Dreamer • Careless Love • I Love You Truly • Let Me Call You Sweetheart • My Gal Sal • Avalon • Frankie and Johnny • Secrets • Margie • Oh By Jingo! • I Want a Girl • Ida • Moonlight Bay • and many more. Arranged in standard C tuning for soprano, concert and tenor ukuleles, with tunes readily adaptable to baritone ukulele, tenor guitars, and guitar-tuned banjos.
00119342...$12.99

HALLELUJAH UKULELE
19 of the Best and Most Beloved Hymns & Spirituals
by Dick Sheridan

Here's a truly special collection of gospel favorites drawn from the traditions of many faiths and cultures. It brings a delightful mix of treasured worship songs, including: Amazing Grace • Go Down, Moses • Hine Mah Tev • In the Garden • The Old Rugged Cross • Rock My Soul • Swing Low, Sweet Chariot • What a Friend We Have in Jesus • and many more. This book contains basic melodies with notes and tablature, exciting creative harmonies, chord symbols and large, easy-to-read diagrams, and selected solos and lyrics.
00122113...$12.99

YULETIDE FAVORITES FOR UKULELE
A Treasury of Christmas Hymns, Carols & Songs
by Dick Sheridan

This holiday collection for uke features easy-to-read arrangements with melody in standard notation, tablature, lyrics, chord symbols and diagrams. Selections include traditional American and English carols as well as songs from other countries. Seasonal and holiday tunes are featured, as well as wassails, ancient airs and dances.
00109749...$9.99

IRISH SONGS FOR UKULELE
by Dick Sheridan

Shamrocks, shillelaghs and shenanigans…they are all here in this collection of 55 fabulous Irish favorites! Each song is specifically arranged for the ukulele, with the melody in both standard notation and easy-to-read tab. Includes: An Irish Lullaby • The Band Played On • Cockles and Mussels • Danny Boy • The Irish Rover • McNamara's Band • Peg O' My Heart • The Rose of Tralee • and dozens more.
00103153...$15.99

COLLEGE FIGHT SONGS & ALMA MATERS FOR UKULELE
by Dick Sheridan

For the varsity football enthusiast, as well as for the perennial college sophomore, here are over 40 of the best-known team songs from major conferneces all across the country in easy-to-play arrangements for the ever-popular ukulele. Even if your own school connection is not included, you'll recognize many of these songs made popular through sporting events, radio and TV broadcasts. Includes arrangements in standard notation and tablature, with lyrics and melodies.
00124458...$15.99

SONGS OF THE CIVIL WAR FOR UKULELE
by Dick Sheridan

25 tunes of the era that boosted morale, championed causes, pulled on the heartstrings, or gave impetus to battle. Includes: All Quiet Along the Potomac, Aura Lee, Battle Hymn of the Republic, Dixie, The Girl I Left Behind Me, John Brown's Body, When Johnny Comes Marching Home and more - all in standard C tuning, with notation, tablature and accompanying lyrics. The book also includes notes on the songs, historical commentary, and a handy chord chart!
00001588...$14.99

P.O. Box 17878 - Anaheim Hills, CA 92817
(714) 779-9390   www.centerstream-usa.com